THE STORY OF
MICROSOFT

ADELE RICHARDSON

A⁺

Published by Smart Apple Media
1980 Lookout Drive, North Mankato, Minnesota 56003

Photography by AP/Wide World (Joe Marquette), Corbis (AFP, Jerry Cooke,
Wolfgang Kaehler, Roger Ressmeyer, Reuters NewMeida Inc.,
Maiman Rick, Doug Wilson), Richard Cummins, Science Photo Library/
Photo Researchers (J.L. Charment, Los Alamos National Laboratory, Volker Steger,
Sheila Terry, Geoff Tompkinson), Unicorn Stock Photos (Martha McBride)

Library of Congress Cataloging-in-Publication Data
Richardson, Adele.
The story of Microsoft / by Adele Richardson.
p. cm. — (Built for success)
Summary: Describes the history of Bill Gates's Microsoft
Corporation and its impact on the computer industry.
Includes bibliographical references.
ISBN 1-58340-294-2
1. Microsoft Corporation—History—Juvenile literature. 2. Computer software
industry—United States—History—Juvenile literature. 3. Microsoft Corporation—
Biography—Juvenile literature. 4. Businessmen—United States—Biography—Juvenile
literature. 5. Gates, Bill, 1955- —Juvenile literature. 6. Jobs, Steven, 1955- —
Juvenile literature. 7. Ballmer, Steven Anthony—Juvenile literature.
[1. Microsoft Corporation—History. 2. Computer software industry.
3. Gates, Bill, 1955- 4. Businesspeople.] I. Title. II. Series.
HD9696.63.U64 M5366 2003
338.7'620053'0973—dc21
2002030901

First Edition
2 4 6 8 9 7 5 3 1

THE STORY OF
MICROSOFT

Table of Contents

Easier and Faster

Microsoft Corporation is one of the biggest and most famous companies in the world. It has brought the personal **computer**, or PC, into the lives of millions of people worldwide. Each year, the company strives to introduce new products for the PC that are more affordable or that are easier to use.

The personal computer has become a vital tool for managing information, and Microsoft played an important role in its development. Authors write books on computers. Accountants work with numbers on computers. Young people play games and do their homework on computers. Individuals around the world can communicate with each other on computers.

Bookkeepers and scientists once required many days or weeks to calculate numbers with paper and pencil. Now computer users can accomplish calculations in a split second—and the answer is always right, provided the user has entered the data correctly. Before personal computers were developed, an author making changes to a book spent weeks retyping the manuscript on a typewriter. Now the author can make changes and reprint the book in a matter of hours.

There is nothing new about finding better ways to handle information. Microsoft has been working on this since 1975. That isn't very long. Human beings have been inventing better ways to handle information for many thousands of years.

Progress in handling information happened slowly. In about 4000 B.C., the Egyptians found a new way to work with numbers. They invented a system of counting using the number 10. That was good progress, but it was not until about 2,000 years later that multiplication tables were invented.

Typewriters have been replaced by computers

Before multiplication tables, figuring out "12 x 12" meant spending a lot of time counting one by one up to 144. In about 1500 B.C.—more than 3,400 years before Microsoft—mathematicians in India invented the mathematical concept of zero. Before that, no one knew how to work with zero as a mathematical idea.

Even though progress was slow, some of the inventions were brilliant. Around 500 B.C., the Babylonians invented the abacus, a faster and easier way of adding and subtracting. It was the first portable counting tool and is still in use today. In fact, some abacus users are faster than many people are on their computers.

In 1642, a French mathematician named Blaise Pascal had an idea that would make his father's work easier. His

father was a tax collector who spent long hours keeping track of who owed taxes and exactly how much they owed. There were a lot of numbers to calculate. Blaise invented a machine that could add and subtract numbers quickly using wheels. He called it the Pascaline.

In 1673, the idea of **binary arithmetic** was invented. A German named Gottfried Leibniz showed that every number could be represented using just two mathematical symbols:

Blaise Pascal (above) was 19 years old when he invented a mechanical calculating machine known as the Pascaline (left)

Charles Babbage never completed his Analytical Engine

zero (0) and one (1). He applied binary arithmetic to the Pascaline computing machine to make it work faster and do more. The Leibniz wheel, as it is now called, could do addition, subtraction, multiplication, and division. Every computer from 1679 until the present has used the binary system.

In the 19th century, Englishman Charles Babbage invented a machine he called the Analytical Engine. It was the world's first fully automatic calculating machine. Babbage's friend, a woman named Augusta Ada, suggested that the Analytical Engine could be programmed using a set of cards that stored information with holes punched in precise places. Every time the machine found a hole in a certain place, it stored, calculated, or printed information depending on where the hole was. Augusta Ada was one of the world's first programmers. She created the **programs** (the holes in the cards) that gave the machine instructions to follow. Unfortunately, Babbage was never able to make the Analytical Engine work.

The Race of Progress

It took thousands of years and a lot of human effort to reach the point at which there was enough information available to invent the Analytical Engine. As technology entered the 20th century, advances began to happen much more quickly.

In 1939, a physicist named John Atanasoff took one of the first steps toward inventing the modern computer. Atanasoff wanted to solve complicated equations more quickly. With the help of a graduate student named Clifford Berry, he used old-fashioned **electronics** and binary arithmetic to build the ABC, or Atanasoff-Berry Computer. The ABC is considered the forerunner of today's **digital** computers.

In 1943, during World War II, the British developed a machine they named Colossus. They used it to break Germany's secret codes. Colossus was the right name for this gigantic machine. It filled a room the size of a small warehouse and contained more than 2,400 **vacuum tubes**. These glass tubes had no oxygen inside, so electricity could flow through them quickly carrying information. Early computers needed a lot of vacuum tubes to manage information.

Early computers consisted of rows of switches and wires

In 1945, soon after the invention of Colossus, the United States Army built ENIAC (Electronic Numeric Integrator and Computer). ENIAC was so fast that it could solve 5,000 addition problems per second. Unfortunately, ENIAC contained 17,468 vacuum tubes, weighed 30 tons (27 t), and was 100 feet (30 m) long by 10 feet (3 m) high. A 1949 issue of *Popular Mechanics* magazine optimistically predicted that one day computers would weigh no more than 1.5 tons (1.4 t).

By 1960, so-called "mini" computers were made that cost $120,000. Less than two years later, vacuum tubes were

ENIAC did not have a screen, keyboard, or mouse

replaced by **transistors**, dramatically reducing the size of the newest computers. By 1964, the cost was down to $18,000, and the mini computer was the size of a refrigerator.

In 1969, Ted Hoff, a researcher at the Intel Corporation, invented tiny **chips** made of silicon that could contain millions of components but were smaller than a fingernail. He placed the silicon chips on **circuit boards**. Four years later, the first personal computer was born.

The Binary System

Inside a modern computer, information is processed using two symbols: zero (0) and one (1). The electrical circuits inside a computer can be turned on and off like a light. A circuit is either on, which is one, or it is off, which is zero.

A user turns the current on and off by inputting data, usually with a keyboard. The computer interprets the data as strings of zeros and ones. Here is how a computer counts from zero to five: 0000=zero, 0001=one, 0010=two, 0011=three, 0100=four, 0101=five. With a string of four digits made up of zeros and ones, 16 possible combinations exist. Each of these combinations can stand for any piece of information the user chooses, such as A equals 0000, B equals 0001, and so on. A computer reads the name "Jackie" as 100100000010101010000100.

This language is called the binary system. The faster a computer's circuits can turn on (one) and off (zero), the faster it can read a name, word, or digit. For example, it turns on and off 24 times to read the name Jackie, 100100000010101010000100.

These are strings of four. If a string of six numbers is used, the possible number of combinations is 64. Computers progressed from using strings of eight numbers (8 bits) to 16 bits and today, strings of 32. That's billions of combinations!

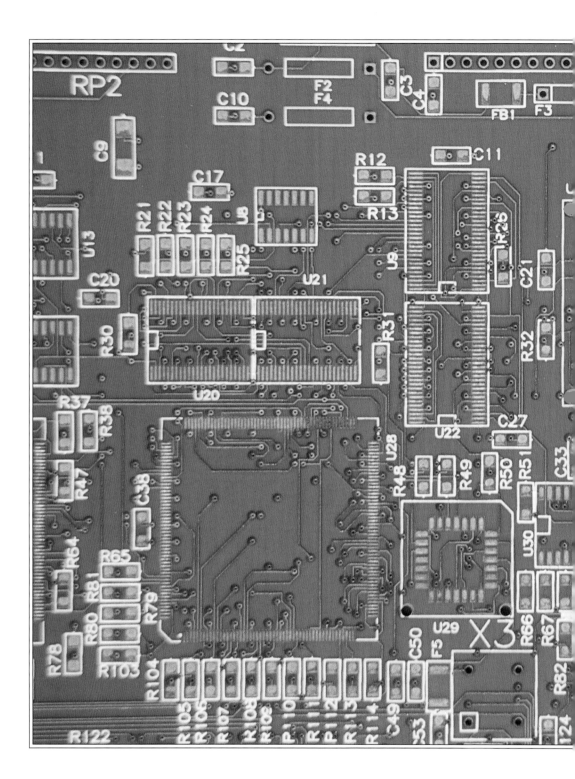

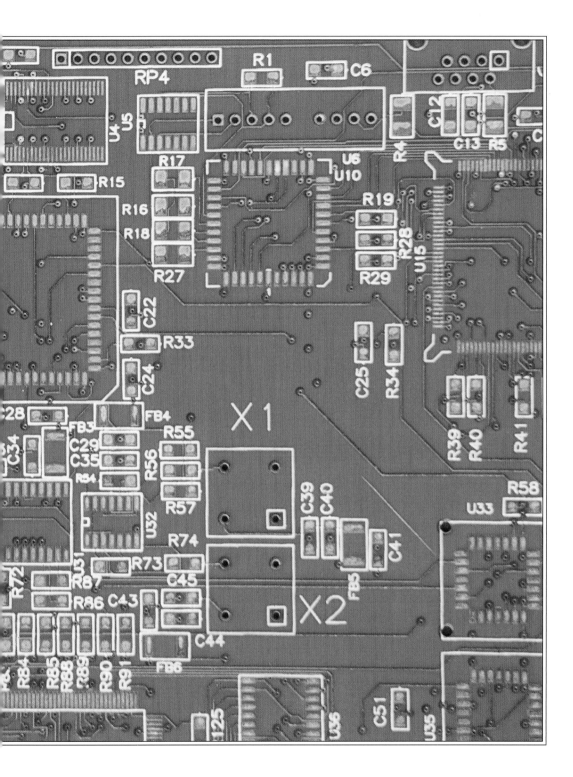

Silicon chips are arranged on circuit boards inside computers

A Computer on Every Desk

Intel's personal computer, with its revolutionary silicon chip and circuit board, had no keyboard or monitor. There were also no programs to tell the computer what to do. Still, people recognized that it had great potential. It could handle all the ones and zeros millions of times faster than the old computers. Unfortunately, there was no way to input data. What Intel's **hardware** needed was **software** to tell it what to do.

All over the world, programmers started creating software for the new computers. These programmers wrote in code, the **language** based on the binary system that computers understand. In 1975, a small company named MITS created the first micro computer. It was smaller and faster than the mini computer. The inventors called it the Altair. Not only was it smaller and faster, it cost only $350. At the time, the personal computer was only a metal box with flashing lights and switches, and no keyboard or monitor. About the only thing users could do with it was play tic-tac-toe. Nonetheless, MITS took 400 orders for the mini computer in just one afternoon. Within three weeks, the company had earned $250,000.

It was clear that people all around the United States were interested in this new technology, but the Altair, like all other computers, needed software. A young man named Bill Gates was a student at Harvard University at the time. His friend Paul Allen worked for an electronics company called Honeywell. The two men developed a version of the computer programming language known as **BASIC**, which stands for Beginner's All-purpose Symbolic Instruction Code. Gates's and Allen's version became known as Altair BASIC.

The Altair BASIC language worked well. It was efficient and easy for programmers to use. Altair BASIC was such a good language that Gates and Allen started Microsoft, a small company dedicated to making software for personal computers. Gates and Allen believed that personal computers would one day become extremely popular in offices and homes. By the end of 1975, Microsoft had earned only $16,000. Nevertheless, Microsoft's two founders were sure that things would change quickly.

In 1976, Altair BASIC caught on with computer enthusiasts. Gates and Allen registered the trade name "Microsoft"

Above, Steve Wozniak co-founded Apple Computers;
left, Apple's first computer; right, Microsoft's Bill Gates

with the Secretary of State in New Mexico. The company

moved into its first real offices in Albuquerque. In July of that

same year, two computer engineers named Steve Wozniak

and Steve Jobs introduced the Apple computer. This new

technology came with a keyboard and could be connected to

a television monitor. It was much more functional than the

Altair, and it quickly gained a reputation for being fun and easy

to use.

Bill Gates: From Programmer to Chairman

William Henry Gates III is the co-founder, **chairman**, and chief software architect of
Microsoft Corporation. He is one of the most influential people in the computer
industry and one of the wealthiest people in the world.

Bill Gates grew up in Seattle, Washington. At age 13 he earned $4,200 for
programming class schedules at a neighborhood school. In 1965, 14-year-old Bill Gates,
his good friend Paul Allen, and two other schoolmates formed the Lakeside Programmers
Group. Their first contract was to write a payroll program for a local business.

When Gates was 15, he and Allen started a company called Traf-O-Data. They used a
computer to track traffic patterns in Seattle and earned $20,000. When he was 17, Gates
took a year off from school to write software programs for a company named TRW.

In 1975, while Gates was attending Harvard University, Paul Allen read an article
about a home computer kit—the Altair 8800. Allen and Gates called the owner of Altair
and told him they were working on a computer language. They signed a contract with
Altair. The two boyhood friends soon formed a partnership they called Microsoft.

Gates, Allen, and Microsoft moved from success to success for many years. Paul
Allen was diagnosed with Hodgkin's disease in 1982, and he left Microsoft the
following year. In the years since then, the company has continued to forge ahead with
Bill Gates at the helm.

But the Apple also needed software. Wozniak and Jobs wanted to include it free of charge with the purchase of their computer. One year later, Microsoft sold the Apple Computer Company a software program called Applesoft BASIC for $21,000. The Apple soon became enormously popular. The company sold more than one million computers—each one with a copy of Applesoft.

In 1977, Microsoft had nine employees and earned $381,715. The next year, the company sold enough software to earn $1,355,655—more than three times the money earned in

Steve Jobs was 21 years old when he co-founded Apple

1977. Allen and Gates decided it was time to head back to the Pacific Northwest, where they had grown up. In 1979, they moved Microsoft to Bellevue, Washington.

In 1980, Microsoft got the break Gates and Allen had hoped for. The fledgling company was asked by International Business Machines (IBM) to provide the languages and **operating system** software for IBM's first personal computers. Microsoft was now supplying vital software to a worldwide giant in the computer industry. A year later, Steve Jobs told Microsoft about Apple's new technology, the Macintosh.

Apple Computers later became Microsoft's main competitor

Microsoft and Apple decided to team up again. Microsoft became the first major company to develop software for the computer that became known as the Mac.

Even though computer users loved the Macintosh, IBM was still the largest, most important company in the industry. Other computer makers wanted their machines to be compatible with IBM machines. Since IBM was using Microsoft's software, these companies also chose Microsoft products. By 1982, Microsoft had hired 220 employees to keep up with the increased demand for its products. Microsoft earned nearly $25 million in 1982.

Now Bill Gates and Paul Allen had to decide whether or not to keep their programming language a secret. If they kept the language exclusively for themselves, companies would have nowhere else to go for their programming. On the other hand, if Gates and Allen shared their programming language, they might make even more money. Potentially, the entire computer industry could work together to create products. By sharing the language, however, Microsoft's founders would have less control over the right to use their ideas.

Gates and Allen made the choices that led to Microsoft's success

Gates and Allen decided to create a common operating system that would make all computers speak the same language. They created MS-DOS (Microsoft Disk Operating System) from a language named Q-DOS that they had purchased from a company called Seattle Computer Products. Then, instead of keeping MS-DOS a secret, Gates and Allen invited other computer programmers to use the system.

This was a very important decision. Thousands of other software companies have been able to use Microsoft programs to develop their own programs for personal computers. This lowers the cost of software for customers and makes a wide range of programs available to the public. Microsoft encourages other companies to write programs for its operating system so that its users have a wide variety of software from which to choose. The popularity of DOS, and later the Windows operating system, has helped to make Microsoft the most successful software company in the world.

The Fast Lane

No one expected Microsoft to grow as quickly as it did. In 1986, the company and its 1,153 employees relocated to the town of Redmond, Washington, near Seattle. That same year, Microsoft went public, which means it began to sell **stock** in the company.

Company leaders expected the five buildings at the new Redmond site to provide enough room for at least the next five years. By 1989, however, Microsoft had more than 4,000 employees. The company needed more space again. Microsoft took over an entire office park, a group of many large buildings that had once been occupied by several different companies. They renamed it Microsoft Place. By 2002, more than 44,000 people worked for Microsoft in 60 countries around the world. More than half of these employees worked at the company's headquarters in Redmond.

Microsoft Corporation is divided into several divisions. A division called Worldwide Sales, Marketing, and Services sells software and offers technical help. The Platforms and Applications division employs software engineers who create

Microsoft always celebrates the introduction of new software

the different operating systems (platforms) and programs (applications). It develops programs for desktop computers, including Microsoft Office for businesses, which has millions of users worldwide.

The Interactive Media division develops software for shopping, entertainment, education, and communication over the **Internet**. It produces an online magazine called *Slate* that can be read on the Internet. It also designs educational CD-ROMs, such as the *Encarta Encyclopedia*. The Interactive Media division teamed up with NBC news to create the 24-hour MSNBC news, talk, and information cable network and Internet service.

Interactive Media also designs computer games such as *3D Movie Maker*, *Impossible Creatures*, and *Flight Simulator 2002*. In 2001, Microsoft's Xbox video game console became available to the public. At the time of its release, the Xbox

Microsoft's Diverse Products

Microsoft sells hundreds of different software programs that perform many different tasks. Computer users can choose Microsoft products that will help them run a business, write a term paper, play a game, or balance the family budget. Microsoft spends billions of dollars every year developing products that make using a computer easier and more efficient. The company's software engineers spend each workday coming up with new ideas that they think computer users need and will enjoy.

Microsoft's beautiful office park is located in Washington state

offered three times the graphics and performance of any other game console on the market. One year later, Xbox Live became available on the Internet. This technology allows players to interact with each other in real time, even though they may be thousands of miles apart.

The Operations division is responsible for giving other companies permission to use Microsoft software. It also deals with the day-to-day concerns of keeping the Microsoft Corporation running smoothly.

As more people use computers, Microsoft keeps growing. To stay successful, Microsoft works hard to do three things. It develops new software quickly, allowing users to do more of the things they want to do with their computers. Secondly, Microsoft makes sure its software is easy to find and sold at reasonable prices. Finally, Microsoft allows other software companies to use its operating system and provides them with the tools they need to develop new programs. The results of Microsoft's strategy are lower costs and a wide range of programs available to computer users.

How Big Is Too Big?

The software industry is growing seven times faster than any other industry in the U.S. The competition is fierce. There are thousands of software companies in the world, and 9 of the 10 largest, including Microsoft, are U.S. companies. Altogether they sold $207 billion worth of software in 2001.

It takes about 12 to 18 months for most hardware or software to become outdated. Software manufacturers must constantly improve their programs in order to stay in business. Microsoft increased spending on research and development of new programs from $2.6 billion in 1997 to $4.3 billion in 2001. It spent more than any other company in the computer industry that year. Even when Microsoft introduces its latest program or operating system, it is already working on the next generation—a newer, more powerful version of the product.

This dedication to staying on top has paid off. In January 2001, Microsoft's Windows operating system controlled 92 percent of the **market share**. This means that 92 percent of computers being used at that time ran using Windows. In recent years, most software companies have designed the majority of

Microsoft released a new version of its operating system in 2001

their programs to work with Windows because it enables them to sell more of their products.

Even the popular Macintosh computer has had a difficult time competing with Windows. Computer users once chose the Macintosh because it was easy to use. The Macintosh operates using the Mac operating system (OS). Microsoft designed Windows using some of the same ideas that made the Macintosh and the Mac OS so popular. Windows became as easy to use as the Mac.

Giving Something Back

Over the years, Bill Gates has donated about $8 million to the Gates Library Foundation. He founded this organization to help North American libraries purchase computer equipment and software. The William H. Gates Foundation was another organization that Gates created and to which he donated millions of dollars. This charity focused on improving the health and education of people worldwide.

In 2000, these two organizations joined to form the Bill and Melinda Gates Foundation. Bill Gates and his wife Melinda have given the foundation more than $21 billion to improve the lives of people around the world.

Gates has also donated all proceeds from his popular books, *The Road Ahead* and *Business @ the Speed of Thought*, to schools and nonprofit organizations.

The Microsoft Corporation does its part as well. Microsoft employees sign up for volunteer programs that benefit many different causes in the Seattle area. The company donates equipment to the same libraries and organizations that receive funds from the Bill and Melinda Gates Foundation.

In 2002, Microsoft Corporation gave away more than $246 million in cash and software to more than 5,000 different nonprofit organizations around the world. Microsoft is the largest contributor to charities in the technology industry and the third highest among all businesses in the U.S.

The Windows system can be used on hundreds of different computer models manufactured by many different companies such as Compaq, Dell, and IBM. The Mac OS can be used only on Apple's Macintosh computers. Programmers began to design more software for Windows and less for the Mac OS. Macintosh sales dropped, and Apple struggled to survive.

In 1997, Microsoft made a $150 million investment in Apple Computer. Many believe this saved Apple from going out of business. Bill Gates and Steve Jobs, Apple's **chief executive officer**, announced a partnership between the two companies. They planned to produce versions of Microsoft Office, Internet Explorer, and other Microsoft tools for the Mac OS.

Now that Microsoft has conquered the PC industry, the company has set its sights on a new frontier: the Internet. In 1995, Gates wrote a best-selling book called *The Road Ahead* in which he explains how important he believes computers and the Internet will be in the future. Computer users now take the Internet and its many uses for granted. Students can research term papers from their desks at home instead of making a trip to the library. International corporations save

Video game players can compete on the Internet using XBox Live

time and money by communicating with partners around the world using e-mail. Media services such as *The New York Times* and the *Associated Press* can pass on the latest news in moments. Companies advertise their products on Web sites. Consumers purchase everything from books to airline tickets using the Internet.

Gates wrote another book in 1999 called *Business @ the Speed of Thought.* In this book, Gates writes about how computers and the Internet can solve business problems and help move information more quickly, as well as improve customer service. In 2002, an estimated 580 million users logged on to the Internet worldwide. Gates believes that people will continue to find exciting new ways to utilize the Internet. Microsoft plans to continue to play an important role in the ongoing Internet revolution.

Gates has said that among the company's biggest goals for the future is to make the Internet easy for everyone to use. "Our framework for this is what I call the Web lifestyle," Gates said. "This is the idea that over the next decade most adults will be using the Web many times a day, without even thinking about it. Now, to make this happen, we're going to have to dramatically improve the technology."

Microsoft's efforts to sell software for the Internet spurred one of the biggest lawsuits in the history of American business. In October 1998, the United States Department of Justice took Microsoft to federal court. It believed Microsoft had broken **antitrust laws**.

In 1996, computer manufacturers sold more than 1,500 new models of computers that ran using the Windows operating system. In its Windows 98 operating system, Microsoft included an **Internet browser** called Microsoft Internet Explorer. This browser automatically came with any computer that ran on the Windows operating system.

The U.S. Department of Justice believed that Microsoft was trying to force other browser companies out of the market. Smaller companies, such as Netscape, simply could not compete in the Internet browser market because Microsoft's product was sold with so many computers. The Justice Department also claimed that Microsoft used its power to force Internet service providers and other companies

Bill Gates defended the way Microsoft conducts business

into exclusive deals using Internet Explorer. This would mean that such companies could use no other browsers.

Microsoft claimed it planned to include Internet Explorer as part of Windows 98 before Netscape and other companies were even founded. The company officials said computer manufacturers included Internet Explorer on their systems because it was a good browser program, not because Microsoft forced them to do so.

At the end of 2001, Microsoft finally reached an agreement with the Justice Department regarding the antitrust lawsuit. According to the settlement, Microsoft is subject to several restrictions on how it develops and sells software for five years. Microsoft must also share information with its competitors about how the software works.

From the beginning, Microsoft has played an important role in the personal computer revolution. The U.S. government and competing computer companies believe Microsoft's role may have become too important. Bill Gates defended Microsoft by saying his company was being punished for its success.

Microsoft leaders have said that complaints about the company's business practices almost always came from its competitors, not its customers. Computer users have made the company a success because they want quality products and innovative ideas at affordable prices. Today Microsoft has the resources and the reputation to attract the best computer engineers who can design the most efficient products. This benefits the customer. As long as Microsoft introduces exciting new products that consumers want, the company will remain a driving force in the computer world.

Microsoft's Pocket PC promises to revolutionize computing

1975 MITS promotes Altair BASIC, a program written by Paul Allen and Bill Gates for the first computer designed for consumers.

1978 Microsoft sales exceed $1 million. Microsoft begins to market its software in Japan.

1981 The IBM personal computer and MS-DOS debut.

1983 The Microsoft Word word-processing program is introduced.

1984 Microsoft produces software for the Apple Macintosh computer.

1985 Microsoft introduces the Windows operating system.

1986 Microsoft goes public and moves to Redmond, Washington.

1987 Microsoft offers 10 reference books on CD-ROM, making CD-ROM technology useful to PC users for the first time.

1989 Microsoft becomes the world's number one software vendor.

1990 Microsoft sales exceed $1 billion. Windows 3.0 is introduced.

1991 Microsoft ships four million copies of Windows 3.0 to 24 countries in 12 different languages.

1995 Windows 95 is released. One million copies are sold in the first four days.

1996 Microsoft creates its Interactive Media division and defines its Internet strategy.

1997 Microsoft invests $150 million in Apple Computers.

1998 Microsoft releases Windows 98. The U.S. Department of Justice files an antitrust complaint against Microsoft.

1999 Microsoft releases Windows 2000.

2000 Gates gives up his title of chief executive officer to Steve Ballmer. He stays at Microsoft as chairman and chief software architect.

2001 Windows XP and the Xbox video game console are released. Microsoft reaches an antitrust settlement with the Justice Department.

antitrust laws Legislation enacted to protect businesses from unfair practices and monopolies. A monopoly is a situation in which one large company has too much control over an industry.

BASIC A simple computer language designed in 1963 by two scientists from Dartmouth University. They created BASIC to be a quick and easy programming language for students and beginning computer users.

binary arithmetic The use of zeros and ones to stand for numbers, letters, and other information.

chairman The person who is in charge of an organization, department, or committee.

chief executive officer The person responsible for managing a company and making decisions that help the company make a profit.

chips Tiny pieces of silicon produced to allow electricity that is carrying information to flow along a path.

circuit boards Arrangements of circuits, or chips, on boards. Chips are inserted onto circuit boards to transfer information inside a computer.

computer A machine designed to store, retrieve, and process information.

digital A way to communicate using binary arithmetic to translate information (such as sounds, words, or pictures) into symbols (zeros and ones). In a computer, those symbols are then sent to a screen and converted back into information for the user to see.

electronics The use of very small amounts of energy, moving in a stream of electricity, to carry information.

GLOSSARY

hardware The electric, metal, and plastic parts of the computer, as opposed to the software programs that run the computer.

Internet A network of computers connected to each other across the world.

Internet browser A software program used to access the Internet.

language The code that computer programmers use to tell a computer what to do. Operating systems and software are created with computer languages.

market share A product's share of the total sales of products of its type.

operating system The basic software that allows a computer to communicate and remember information. An operating system also allows other application programs to work together.

programs Series of instructions supplied to a computer so it can complete a task.

software The program or operating system that tells a computer's hardware what to do.

stock Shared ownership in a company by many people who buy shares, or portions, of stock, hoping that the company will make a profit so that their shares will increase in value.

transistors Small devices that control electric current.

vacuum tubes Glass tubes with all the air removed so electricity can flow through them easily in order to pass information through a system electronically. Vacuum tubes were used as electrical circuits in computers before the development of the transistor and silicon chip.

INDEX

INDEX

Books

Barton-Wood, Sara. *Bill Gates: Computer Giant.* Austin, Tex.: Raintree Steck-Vaughn, 2002.

Dunn, John M. *The Computer Revolution. (World History Series.)* San Diego, Calif.: Lucent Books, 2002.

Graham, Ian. *The Internet Revolution. (Science at the Edge.)* Chicago, Ill.: Heinemann Library, 2002.

Lee, Lauren. *Bill Gates.* Milwaukee, Wisc.: World Almanac Library, 2002.

Web Sites

Computer History Museum
http://www.computerhistory.org

Internet Society: All About the Internet
http://www.isoc.org/internet/history

Official Web Site of the Microsoft Corporation
http://www.microsoft.com

Triumph of the Nerds: A History of the Computer
http://www.pbs.org/nerds/timeline